I'd like to give an enormous thank you to Jodi, my life long best friend. She is an amazing person; as a wife, mother and artist. She agreed to collaborate on this book with me and was able to bring my words to life. Her beautiful watercolor illustrations generated the feelings and emotions I was looking for, all without my guidance. This is just one reason why I call her my 'soul sister'.

Copyright © 2014 Jennifer L. Young • All rights reserved.

The creation of this book is dedicated to God, for without Him, the spirit wouldn't have moved me to write it. I thank God for my parents, Margaret and Francis Young. Without their unconditional love and support I would not be the woman I am today. They have been my foundation on which to stand and encourage me to display my talents to the world but more importantly have kept me from falling during times when I faltered. I thank God for blessing me with my sister, Stephanie. She has brought joy and laughter to my world in times she didn't even realize I needed it. God has blessed us all with people who have Down Syndrome. They have the ability to teach everyone what absolute love, support and trust is truly meant to be. We just need to open our hearts and minds to learn from them, just like Stephanie continues to teach me.

Once upon a time many years ago,

A man and a woman met, their love began to grow.

A few years after dating they decided to get married,

Not much time passed and a baby the woman carried.

Back then doctors had no way to know if it would be a girl or a boy,

    But these parents didn't care because they were just filled with joy.

Seven months later a baby girl was born early,

    She seemed to be healthy and her hair was so curly.

The doctor had news for the parents he didn't want to share,

    For their baby girl was born with Down Syndrome and would need much care.

He explained to both of them that no one was to blame,

But it didn't matter as the mothers' tears came.

The doctor also said she may live to be only a year,

As you can imagine, this brought them many fears.

He reminded them they didn't do anything wrong,

So they named her Stephanie and took her home.

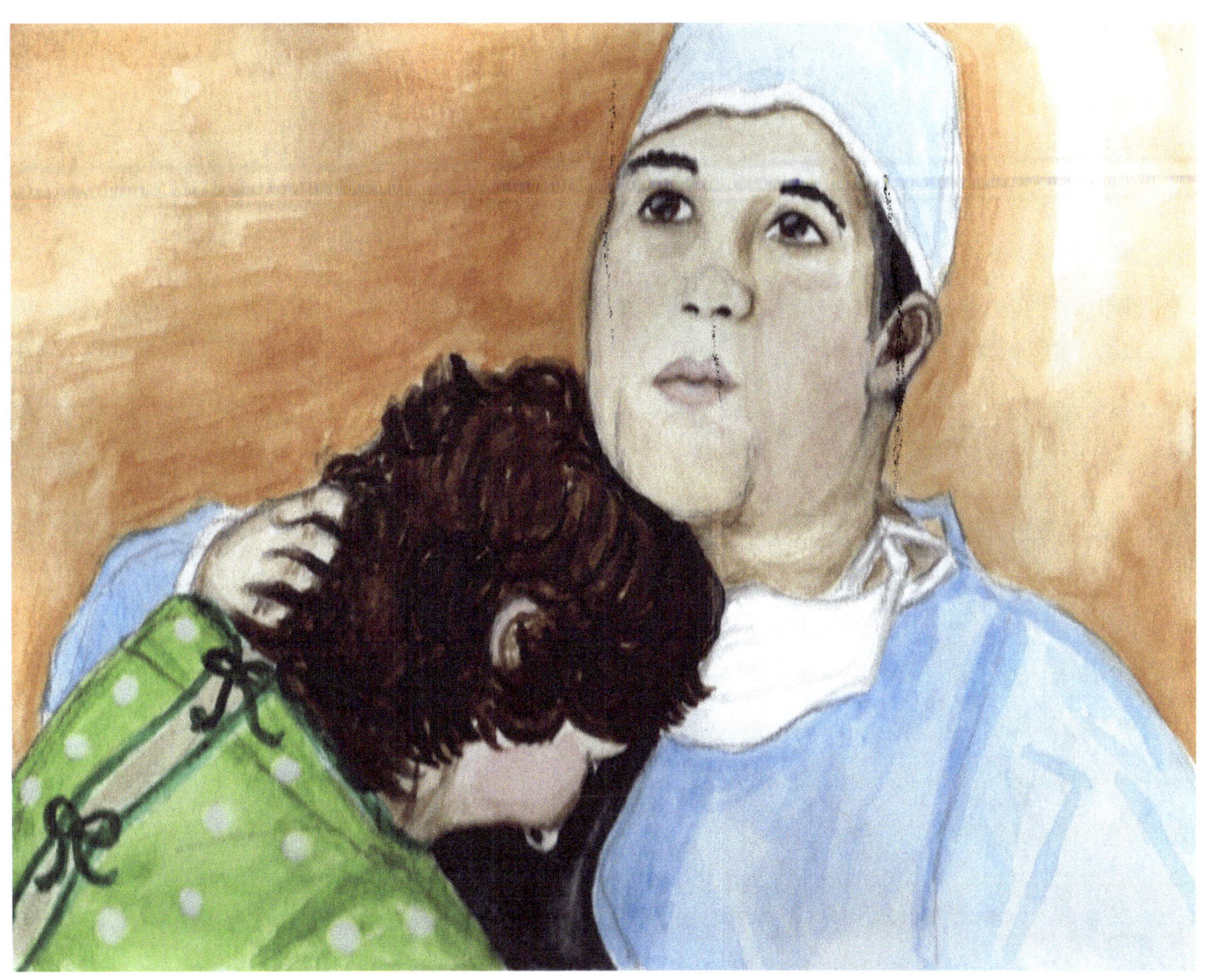

Stephanie's first birthday was soon to arrive,

    Her parents were grateful but wondered if she'd make it to five.

As she was growing she often got sick,

    The doctor gave her medicine and fixed her up quick.

Well, Stephanie turned five so the parents thought awhile,

    Maybe they should have another baby, this thought made them smile.

Nine months later another girl the parents had,

> The doctor said she was healthy and this news made them glad.

They called her Jennifer, a beautiful name,

> "Thank God she's healthy", both parents exclaimed.

Now Stephanie had a baby sister to have fun with and play,

> It was hard for her to be patient; she couldn't wait for that day.

When Jennifer was old enough she knew Stephanie was special,

      But at the time she didn't know she was in for a handful.

They started out playing like normal sisters did,

      They'd dress up their dolls or go seek while the other one hid.

They sat together to color and made up silly songs to sing,

On beautiful sunny days they would be out on the swings.

You could find them in the sandbox or blowing up balloons,

At night they'd catch fireflies and stare at the moon.

Eventually they started to ride the same bus to school,

Stephanie would tell fake stories about her not knowing it was cruel.

It wasn't until then Jennifer was noticing the difference,

Her sister wasn't as normal as she thought, it didn't make sense.

She began to get upset with Stephanie and wished there was a cure,

Couldn't the doctors take the Down Syndrome away from her?

Every year Stephanie got three birthday parties and Jennifer got one,

> She started to wonder what was wrong, what had she done?

When her parents felt she was old enough they left Stephanie in her care,

> Jennifer would miss sleep overs with friends, it became more than she could bear.

None of this was fair since Stephanie was older,

> Jennifer kept silent even though her heart grew colder.

On days their parents were at work and she took care of her sister,

> Jennifer would get mad; she would bite and even hit her.

A few times she got so mad and told her parents she hated them, even slammed her bedroom door in their face,

> She cried to herself "why can't I have a normal sister? I want out of this place!"

Eventually she decided to keep her feelings bottled up inside,

> She didn't want attention taken away from Stephanie, she had too much pride.

As they grew older the fighting eventually stopped,

    Jennifer felt guilty and knew her actions had gone over the top.

Some nights she questioned God about why He didn't give her a 'normal' sister,

    Although at the same time if she wasn't around, she knew she would miss her.

There were moments Jennifer wanted to ask her parents, "Am I special too?"

    Then again if their answer was 'no' than what would she do?

She knew in her heart Stephanie needed more care,

So when she felt sad she went to God in prayer.

She begged God to make her not feel this way,

She would kneel on the floor as she began to pray.

Jennifer never got an answer or maybe didn't hear,

For God created her also with tender loving care.

As time went on Jennifer left home to get an education,

> Maybe this would help her feel better, not living in the situation.

It wasn't until she was at college, away from her family,

> She heard God say, "My child have patience, My plan you will see".

Her senior year in college Jennifer had to write a paper about her life,

> It wasn't until then she understood her parents raised her just right.

The light bulb finally went off in her head,

    She was special too no matter what anyone said.

She let go of her bad feelings and threw them away,

    It was then a new love for her family started to grow on that day.

Jennifer knows if she asked her parents today,

"Am I special too?" just what they would say.

"You are also very special; we have loved you every day,

And just like Stephanie, we love you the same way".

www.ingramcontent.com/pod-product-compliance
Lightning Source LLC
Chambersburg PA
CBHW060531010526
44110CB00052B/2564